[redacted]

WHS

national TESTS
revision guide

Science

revision guide

10–11

YEARS

Key Stage 2

[redacted]

First published 2000
exclusively for WHSmith by

Hodder & Stoughton Educational
338 Euston Road
LONDON NW1 3BH

A CIP record for this book is available from the British Library.

Text: Richard Barnett
Illustrations: Clive Wakfer
Developed by Topics The Creative Partnership Ltd, Exeter

ISBN 0-340-78991-3

10 9 8 7 6 5 4 3 2 1

Printed and bound in Great Britain for Hodder & Stoughton Educational by
Hobbs the Printers, Totton, Hants.

Contents

Introduction

The *Revision Guide* series

National Tests Revision Guides are a new series of books that take an exciting visual approach to revision for National Tests. Each topic is summarised in a chart to help your child see it as a whole, remember key ideas and understand the links between them. This book is a Science revision guide for children in Years 3 to 6 of primary school who are working through Key Stage 2. It is especially targeted at children approaching the tests that all pupils have to take at the end of Key Stage 2.

Attainment Targets and levels

The content of each subject in the National Curriculum is divided into a series of target areas. These are called Attainment Targets. An example of an Attainment Target in Science is Life Processes and Living Things.

Each Attainment Target is divided into eight levels and the National Curriculum provides a detailed description of the skills and knowledge which a child should be displaying at each level. So, during the learning process it may be said that some children are working at a particular level and others are working towards a particular level (but have achieved the one below).

On average, children are expected to advance one level for every two years they are at school. By the end of Key Stage 2, when they are 10–11 years old, most children should have reached level 4, although some may be working at levels 3, 5, or 6. The diagram below shows the range of levels at the ends of Key Stages 1, 2 and 3.

- □ Exceptional performance
- ■ Exceeded targets for age group
- ○ Achieved targets for age group (working at)
- ● Working towards targets for age group

	Level 8+	Level 8	Level 7	Level 6	Level 5	Level 4	Level 3	Level 2	Level 1
7 years						□	■	○	●
11 years				□	■	○	●	●	●
14 years	□	■	■	○	○	●	●	●	●

The National Tests

The National Tests (also known as SATs) are intended to let parents, children and teachers know how the child is doing in relation to National Curriculum Attainment Targets. They are designed to find what level of attainment a child has reached in the core subjects of English, Mathematics and (from Key Stage 2 onwards) Science. The score that a child achieves is converted directly into a level. This is the result that is given to children and parents (or other carers).

About this guide

This guide covers the key points and main ideas of Science at Key Stage 2. It revises work done by children in class and does not attempt to teach new material from scratch.

Each important topic occupies a single page or double-page spread. Some key points are listed at the top of the page. These are then expanded in the chart below, showing how ideas are linked. The margins contain further information, ideas for children to try out to help them improve their knowledge and skills in Science and advice on revision methods. Illustrations also aid visual memory.

It is not intended that children should work through the book from start to finish. Rather, the book is a resource to dip into to find out more about particular topics. Topics that the child finds difficult can be revisited as many times as necessary.

The chart can be used by the child in a variety of ways:

- learning a small section at a time, covering up the section and checking if they know the main words and ideas;
- writing out some of the main ideas as sentences or diagrams;
- checking out any ideas they did not know in their textbook or by asking a teacher;
- following a process in the chart as they practise examples, especially in English or Mathematics.

WHSmith also publishes an extensive range of *National Tests Practice Papers*, which make an excellent companion to this series.

Features of this guide

Revision tips and activities.

This section tells you the key ideas your child needs to know and understand.

The main part of the page builds on the key ideas and shows how they relate to one another.

- It provides examples of how the key ideas work.
- It gives more explanation of the key ideas.
- It gives meanings of main words or processes involved.

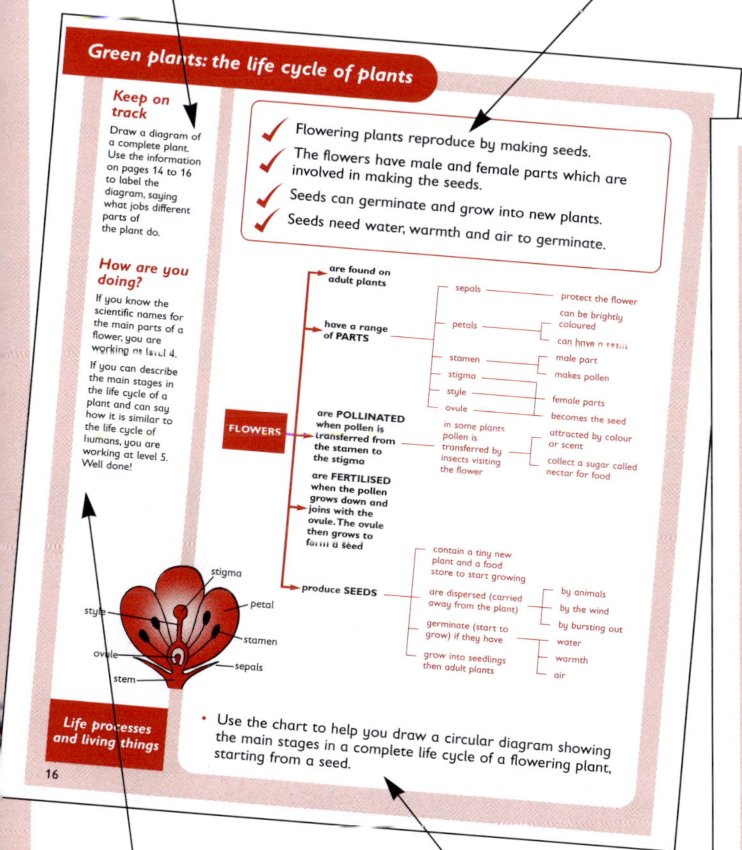

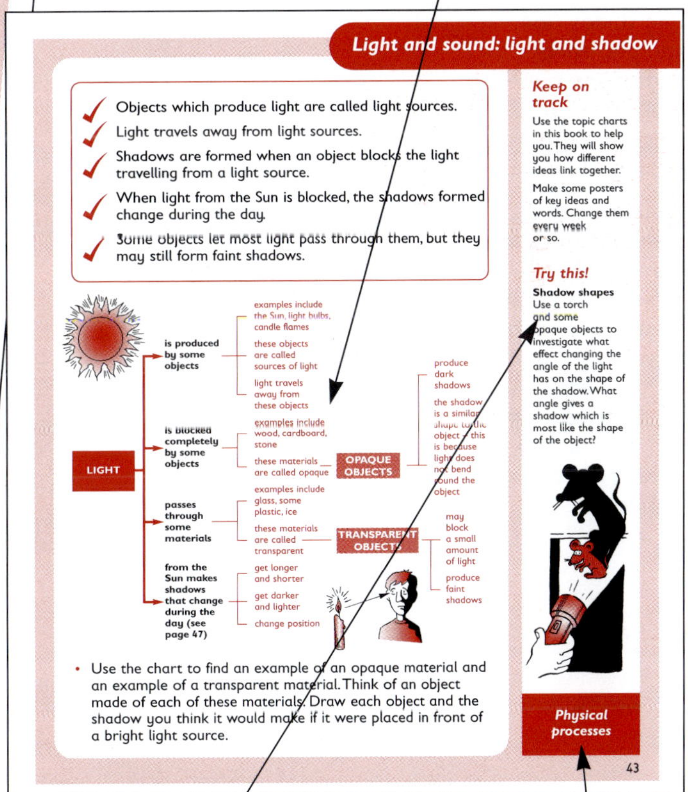

Uses examples from the topic to indicate which level your child is working at.

Activity or trigger question to encourage your child to find and use information in the chart.

Ideas to help your child practise or expand his or her knowledge and skills.

Tells you the Attainment Target.

Keep on track

Growth, feeding, reproduction and movement are the main life processes in plants and animals. Can you make up a sentence with words starting with the same first letters to help you remember these processes?

How are you doing?

If you can say how living things are different from non-living things (for example, living things grow but non-living things don't), you are working at level 3.

If you know the scientific names for the main life processes in plants and animals, such as reproduction and nutrition, and you can describe what each means, you are working at level 4. Well done!

- ✓ All animals reproduce, grow and move. To do this they need food and water.
- ✓ All plants reproduce and grow. To do this they need food and water.
- ✓ Animals take in food and water in their diet.
- ✓ Green plants can make food by using water and air when they are in the light.

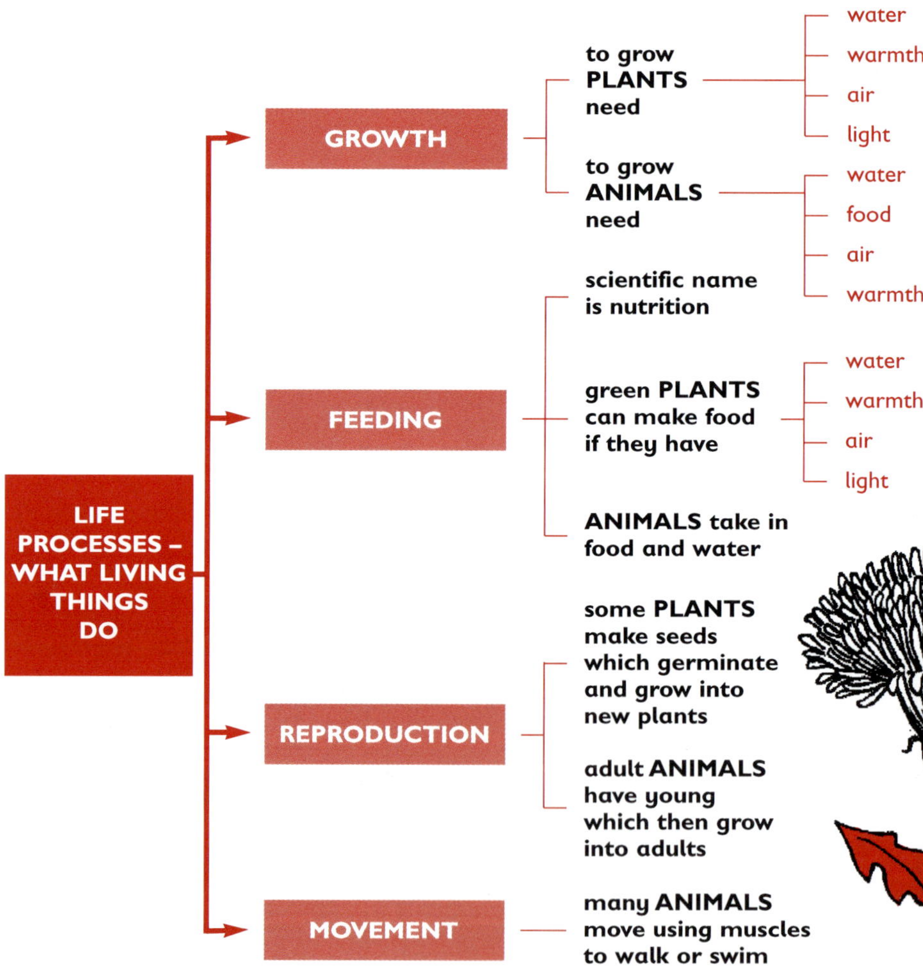

- Use the chart to make a list of the life processes that are found in both plants and animals. Now work out three differences between the processes in plants and animals.

Life processes and living things

- ✓ Teeth help to break down the food we eat.
- ✓ Humans have different types of teeth which break down the food in different ways.
- ✓ Humans have two sets of teeth during their lives.
- ✓ Humans have to take care of their teeth.

TEETH

- **humans have different TYPES of teeth**
  - **INCISORS**
    - have sharp edges
    - cut up food
    - are at the front of the mouth
  - **CANINES**
    - are pointed teeth
    - tear food
    - are at the side of the mouth
  - **PRE-MOLARS AND MOLARS**
    - are square teeth
    - chew the food
    - are at the back of the mouth
- **humans have two SETS of teeth**
  - **MILK TEETH** — the first set can last until the person is about nine years old
  - **ADULT TEETH** — the second set can last for the rest of the person's life
- **need to be looked after to stay HEALTHY**
  - **BRUSHING**
    - keeps the teeth clean
    - keeps the gums healthy
  - **TOO MANY SWEET FOODS CAN MAKE THE TEETH DECAY**

- When you eat an apple, which types of teeth are used and what jobs do they do? Use the chart to work out the answer. Think of three other foods and decide which types of teeth you use to eat them.

Keep on track

Look in the mirror and draw a picture of your own teeth. Use the information in the chart to label the different types of teeth!

Try this!

Work out your top five tips for keeping healthy teeth and gums. Check if the advice given on toothbrush and toothpaste packets is the same. What does your dentist think?

Keep on track

Why not draw up a timetable for your revision? This will help you to decide which topics to revise each night.

Tick off sections on your revision timetable as you cover them. Aim to cover each topic at least twice before the tests.

Try this!

Does everybody in your family need the same food? Write down the names of some of the people in your family and decide who needs the most food for growth and who needs the most food for activity.

- ✓ All animals, including humans, need to take in food.
- ✓ Animals need food for growth.
- ✓ Some foods are a good source of the materials which animals need for growth.
- ✓ Animals need food for activity.
- ✓ Some foods are a good source of energy for activity.

FOOD for

- **GROWTH**
  - **these TYPES OF FOOD are important for growth**
    - fish, meat, cheese, beans — contain protein
    - children need plenty of these foods in their diet
- **ACTIVITY**
  - **these TYPES OF FOOD are important for activity**
    - rice, potatoes, pasta — contain starch
    - fruit — contains sugar
    - everyone needs these foods to provide energy for movement
  - **these TYPES OF FOOD also provide energy**
    - chocolate, sweets, cakes — contain fats and sugar
      - too much of these can be bad for you

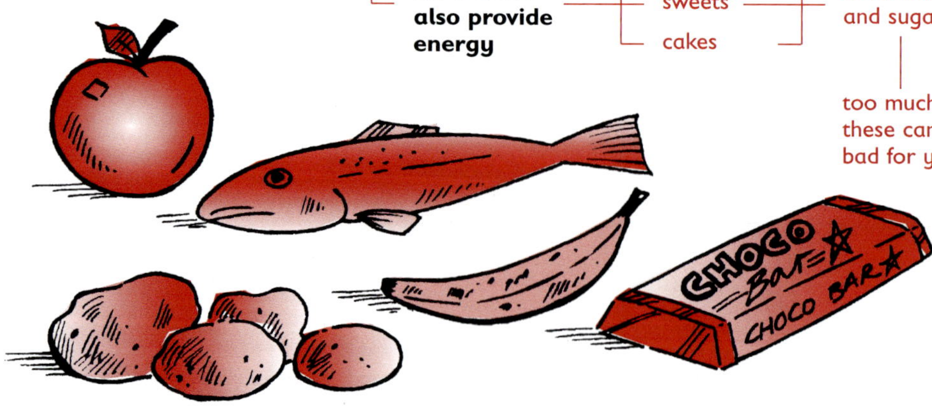

- Use the chart to find out three types of food that you must eat enough of.

- To stay healthy, humans need a diet that contains enough food and water.
- To stay healthy, humans need a varied diet.
- To stay healthy, humans need the right balance of different kinds of food in their diet.
- Different types of animal need different diets to keep them healthy.

DIET AND HEALTH

- **a person's DIET is the food and drink that they take in**
  - some people choose to eat different types of diet, e.g. vegetarian
  - different animals need different types of diet, e.g. dogs – mainly meat, sheep – all plant material
- **a person's diet must have ENOUGH food and water**
  - for growth
  - for activity
  - to keep the body working
- **a person's diet must have enough VARIETY**
  - fruit, vegetables — for energy, for vitamins, for fibre
  - fish, meat, beans, cheese — for growth, for vitamins
  - bread, pasta — for energy, for fibre
- **a person's diet must be BALANCED** — enough of each type of food, but not too much
  - food for growth
  - food for energy
  - food with vitamins
  - fat — can make you overweight
  - sugar — too much is bad for you

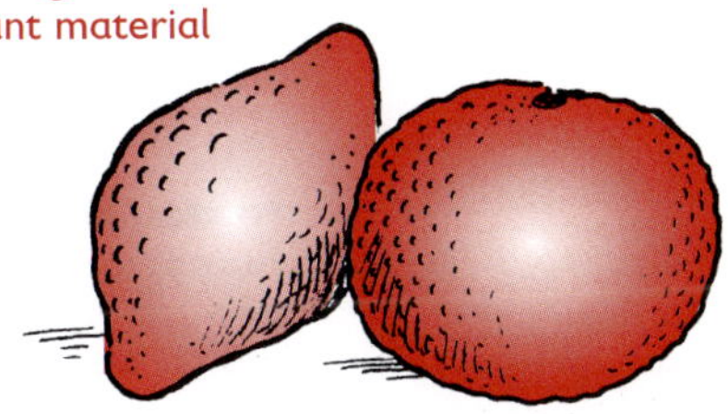

- Work out the menus for three meals that you could eat during a day to give you a varied and balanced range of foods. Use the chart to help you.

Keep on track

Write out two sets of cards – one set listing examples of foods and the other set saying what food can provide, e.g. energy or fibre. Match each food card with the right cards from the second set.

Try this!

Vitamin C is found in many fruits and vegetables. Make a list of foods which you like that you think would be a good source of vitamin C in your diet. Check if you were right by looking at food packaging, information leaflets in supermarkets or in books. Do any of these sources of information tell you why vitamin C is important in the diet?

Humans and other animals: a healthy body

Keep on track

Make up a crossword about keeping your body healthy. Try the crossword out on a friend.

How are you doing?

If you know the scientific names for the parts of the body that you have studied (for example, the heart, the skull and the spine), you are working at level 4.

If you can describe how the parts of the body that you have studied work (for example, the heart or the skeleton), you are working at level 5. Well done!

- ✓ Humans need exercise to keep their muscles healthy.
- ✓ Exercise helps to keep the heart and lungs healthy.
- ✓ Drugs are substances that can change how the body works.
- ✓ Some drugs can be very harmful to the body.
- ✓ Some drugs, taken as medicines, can help the body if we use them correctly.

A HEALTHY BODY

- **to stay healthy humans need a balanced DIET – look at the chart on page 9**
- **to stay healthy humans need enough EXERCISE which affects**
  - the muscles
    - work harder when we exercise
    - over time become stronger
  - the heart
    - beats faster when we exercise to pump more blood to the muscles
    - with regular exercise the heart becomes stronger
  - the lungs
    - with regular exercise lungs are able to take in more air
    - we breathe faster and more deeply when we exercise to take in oxygen
- **DRUGS**
  - can be helpful to the body
    - if taken as medicine when we are ill
    - if they are taken
      – at the right time
      – in the right amounts
  - can be harmful to the body
    - if they damage the body – for example, tobacco damages the lungs
    - if they change how a person behaves – for example, alcohol affects behaviour

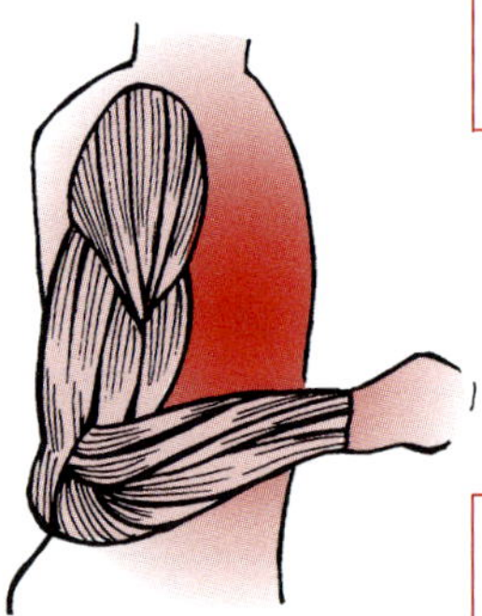

- Use the chart to identify three parts of the body that are affected by exercise. Explain how exercise helps each of these parts of the body.

- The heart pumps blood around the body.
- The heart is made of muscle which contracts to pump the blood.
- The blood is carried to all parts of the body in tubes called blood vessels.
- We can feel the blood going through some of the vessels when the heart beats. This is called the pulse.
- When we exercise, the heart beats faster so the pulse feels quicker.

THE HEART

- is found in the chest and is **PROTECTED BY**
  - the ribs
  - the chest bone

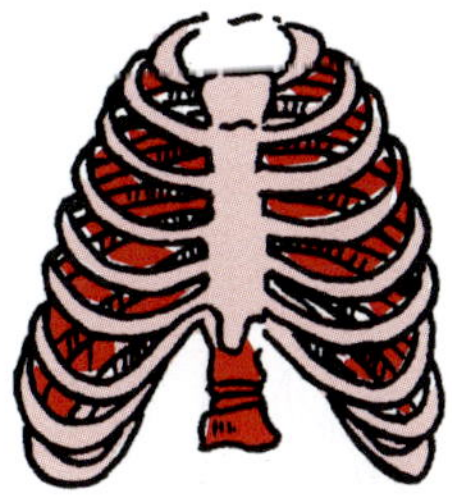

- is made of muscle which **CONTRACTS** when the heart pumps
  - the contractions can be felt
    - in the chest as the heart beat
    - in the wrist and neck as a pulse
- **PUMPS the BLOOD**
  - round the body in tubes called blood vessels
  - to the lungs to pick up oxygen
  - to all other parts of the body to carry the oxygen and food
  - faster when we exercise to carry more food and oxygen to the muscles so they can work harder

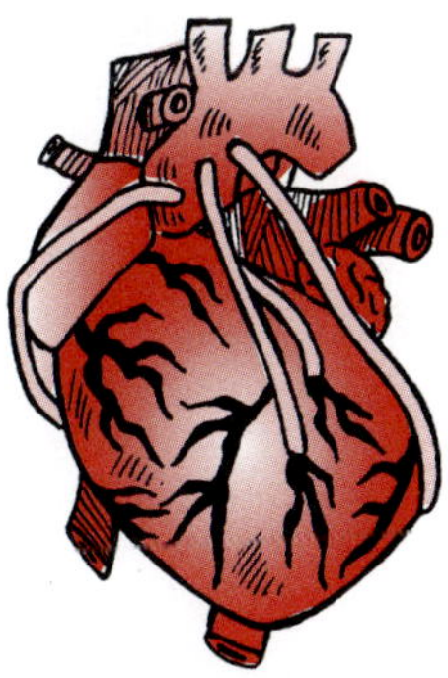

- Use the chart to work out what happens to the heart when we exercise and explain why this happens.

Keep on track

Don't just read the work. Make your revision active by doing tasks such as changing the text into a diagram.

If you are trying to remember key words, write them out, cover them up and try to write them again. Then check your new list against the first one.

Try this!

Exercise will make your heart beat faster but does the position of your body change how fast your heart beats? Investigate your pulse rate when you are standing up, sitting down and lying down. What about taking readings for some other people to compare with yours: is there a pattern in the results?

Humans and other animals: support and movement

Keep on track

Work with a friend. Point to different parts of your body and try to name the bone found there. Check your answers in your science book.

Try this!

The human skeleton contains more than 200 bones! How many separate bones can you feel in your body? Why are some bones difficult to find? Use a diagram or a skeleton model to help you work this out.

- ✓ Humans and some other animals have a skeleton inside their bodies which is made of bones.
- ✓ The skeleton grows as the person or animal grows.
- ✓ The bones in the skeleton support the body and some protect delicate parts of the body such as the brain.
- ✓ Muscles are fastened to the bones in the skeleton. The muscles can pull on the bones and make the body move. Muscles are arranged in pairs.

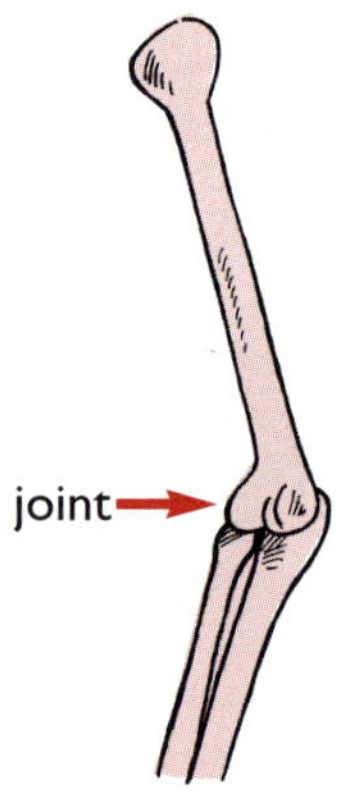

THE HUMAN SKELETON

- **is made up of BONES which are**
  - hard
  - strong
  - smooth
  - linked by joints
- **the bones have NAMES**
  - skull
  - ribs
  - spine
  - jaw
  - femur (thigh bone)
- **some parts of the skeleton PROTECT the body**
  - skull — brain
  - ribs — lungs
  - chest bone — heart
- **supports and helps the body to MOVE**
  - the arms and legs have long bones
  - muscles can contract to move the bones
  - when one muscle contracts the opposite muscle relaxes
  - the bones are connected by joints which can bend

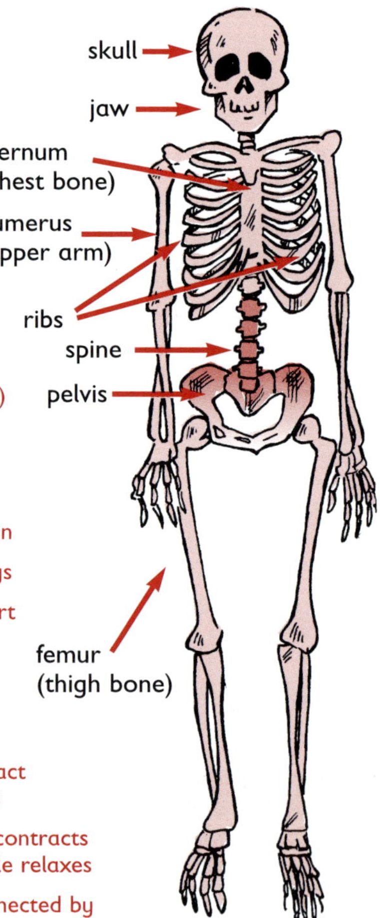

- The skeleton has two important jobs. Use the chart to decide what they are.

Humans and other animals: the life cycle of humans

- ✓ Humans reproduce by having babies.
- ✓ Human babies grow and develop through stages to become adults.
- ✓ Human babies and children need help from their parents for several years.

HUMANS

- **male and female adult humans reproduce to make babies**
- **grow and develop through several STAGES**
  - **UNBORN BABY develops inside the mother – 9 months**
    - gets food and warmth inside the mother
  - **BABY up to 2 years old**
    - gets bigger
    - learns to walk
    - starts to talk
    - needs its parents to feed and dress it
  - **CHILD between about 2 and 12 years old**
    - grows steadily
    - goes to school
    - learns to read and write
    - needs parents to help with decisions
  - **ADOLESCENT between about 12 and 18 years old**
    - may grow quickly
    - body changes to become an adult
    - much more independent of parents
    - may leave home
  - **ADULT between about 18 and 80 years old**
    - finishes growing
    - may start work
    - may have a family
    - when very old may need support from other adults

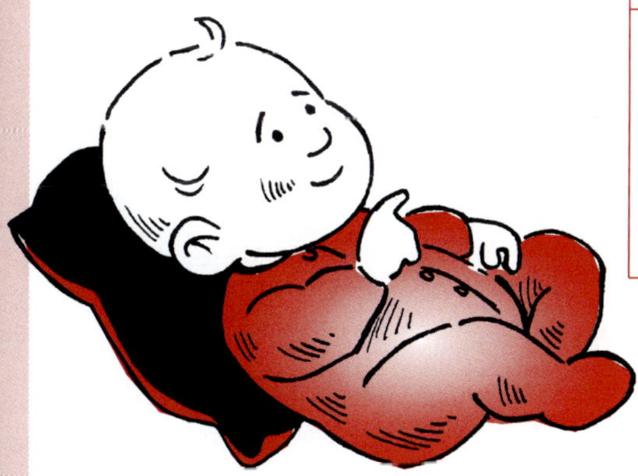

- Use the chart to make a table which shows the stages in a person's life and some of the things that the person will learn to do at each stage in their life.

Keep on track

Start revising with a blank piece of paper. Write down what you already know about a topic. Then revise the bits you missed out!

Draw a chart like the ones in this book to record what you already know about a topic.

Use the charts in this book to add to the ones you have already made.

Try this!

Humans look after their children for a long time, but how do other animals look after their young? Make a list of five different types of animal and try to find out how the adult animals look after their young.

Green plants: leaves and growth

Keep on track

Practise test questions whenever you can. Use WHSmith's *National Tests Practice Papers*.

Allow some time in your revision plan to practise drawing diagrams and graphs.

Try this!

Plant-growing competition
With some friends or your family buy some small plants. Take a plant each and try to give it the best possible conditions for growth. After a few weeks either measure the height of the plants or weigh the crop to decide the winner. (Tomato plants would be good for this idea but try to get identical ones to start with so the competition is fair.)

Life processes and living things

- ✓ To grow well, green plants need the right amount of water.
- ✓ To grow well, green plants need warmth.
- ✓ To grow well, green plants need light.
- ✓ In the light, green plants can use water and air to make new materials.
- ✓ Plants make the new material in their leaves.

GREEN PLANTS

- **need WATER to grow**
  - plants need water to make food
  - if they don't have enough water plants don't grow very well
  - if they have too much water plants can die
- **need AIR to grow**
  - usually plants have plenty of air around them
  - air gets into plants through tiny holes in the leaves
  - plants use a gas called carbon dioxide from the air when they make food
- **need WARMTH to grow**
  - in a low temperature plants grow slowly
  - if the temperature is too high plants may die
- **need LIGHT to grow**
  - plants need enough light to grow well
  - when it is light the leaves can use water and carbon dioxide in the air to make new material for the plant
    - this is how green plants make food for growth
    - light energy is needed to make this process happen
    - this process is called photosynthesis

- Use the chart to make two lists, one which shows the substances a plant needs to grow well and one which shows the surroundings the plant has to be in to grow well.

Green plants: water and roots

- ✓ The roots of a plant help to anchor it into the ground.
- ✓ The roots of a plant take in water and some nutrients.
- ✓ Water is carried up the stems of plants to the leaves.

WATER IN PLANTS

- **is taken in from the soil by the ROOTS**
  - some plant roots spread to find water
  - some plant roots go deep in the ground to find water
- **these take in small amounts of substances called MINERALS with the water**
  - minerals are sometimes called nutrients
  - minerals are found in fertilizers added to the soil to help plants grow
  - minerals are needed, together with the food made in the leaves, for plant growth
- **travels up the STEM of the plant to the LEAVES**
  - small tubes in the stem carry the water
  - most of the water escapes into the air through tiny holes in the leaves
  - some of the water is used in the leaves when the plant makes food – look at the chart on page 14

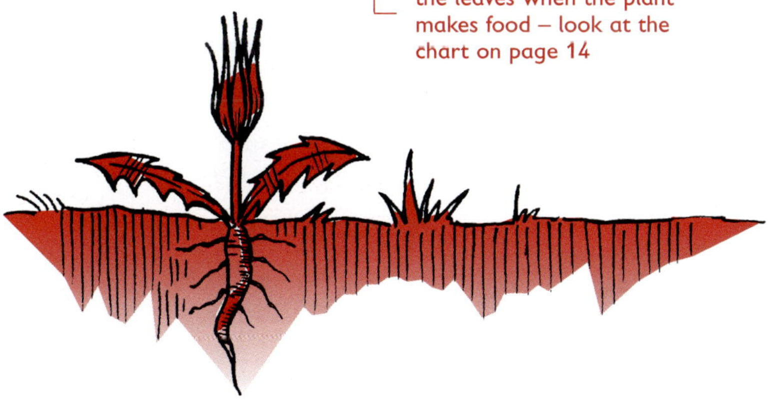

- Use the chart to describe the journey of water through a plant. Could the journey end in different places?

Keep on track

Use the topic charts in this book to help you. They will show you how the different ideas link together.

Make a mega chart Try to find ideas that link topics together to produce larger charts.

Make up some questions to test your friends with – this helps you to understand the ideas involved.

Try this!

Try putting a small, well-watered potted plant into a sealed polythene bag overnight. Where do you think the water on the inside of the bag comes from? Can you improve the design of the experiment to prove that the water found on the inside of the bag must have escaped from the leaves of the plant?

Green plants: the life cycle of plants

Keep on track

Draw a diagram of a complete plant. Use the information on pages 14 to 16 to label the diagram, saying what jobs different parts of the plant do.

How are you doing?

If you know the scientific names for the main parts of a flower, you are working at level 4.

If you can describe the main stages in the life cycle of a plant and can say how it is similar to the life cycle of humans, you are working at level 5. Well done!

- ✓ Flowering plants reproduce by making seeds.
- ✓ The flowers have male and female parts which are involved in making the seeds.
- ✓ Seeds can germinate and grow into new plants.
- ✓ Seeds need water, warmth and air to germinate.

FLOWERS

- **are found on adult plants**
- **have a range of PARTS**
  - sepals — protect the flower
  - petals
    - can be brightly coloured
    - can have a scent
  - stamen
    - male part
    - makes pollen
  - stigma, style, ovule — female parts
  - ovule — becomes the seed
- **are POLLINATED when pollen is transferred from the stamen to the stigma**
  - in some plants pollen is transferred by insects visiting the flower
    - attracted by colour or scent
    - collect a sugar called nectar for food
- **are FERTILISED when the pollen grows down and joins with the ovule. The ovule then grows to form a seed**
- **produce SEEDS**
  - contain a tiny new plant and a food store to start growing
  - are dispersed (carried away from the plant)
    - by animals
    - by the wind
    - by bursting out
  - germinate (start to grow) if they have
    - water
    - warmth
    - air
  - grow into seedlings then adult plants

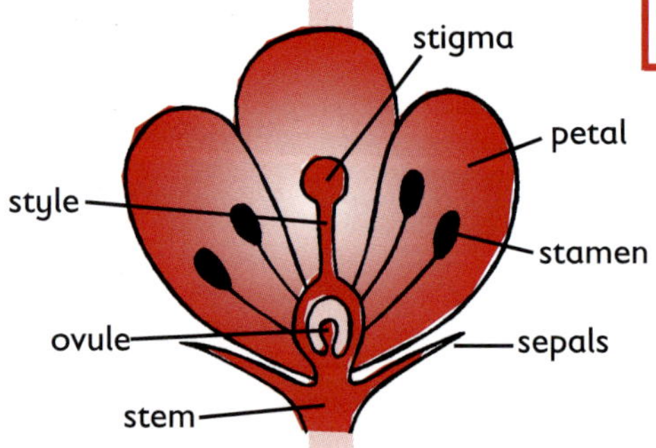

Life processes and living things

- Use the chart to help you draw a circular diagram showing the main stages in a complete life cycle of a flowering plant, starting from a seed.

- ✓ Animals and plants can be put into groups.
- ✓ The groups depend on the differences you can see between the plants or animals.
- ✓ A key is a series of questions which helps you to decide which group a plant or an animal belongs in.

IDENTIFYING PLANTS AND ANIMALS

FEATURES OF PLANTS AND ANIMALS
- looking carefully at plants and animals can help you identify them
- features of plants and animals which can be seen are called observable features
- observable features for animals include:
  - – number of legs
  - – wings or no wings
  - – type of coat
- observable features for plants include:
  - – colour of flower
  - – shape of leaves
  - – colour of stem

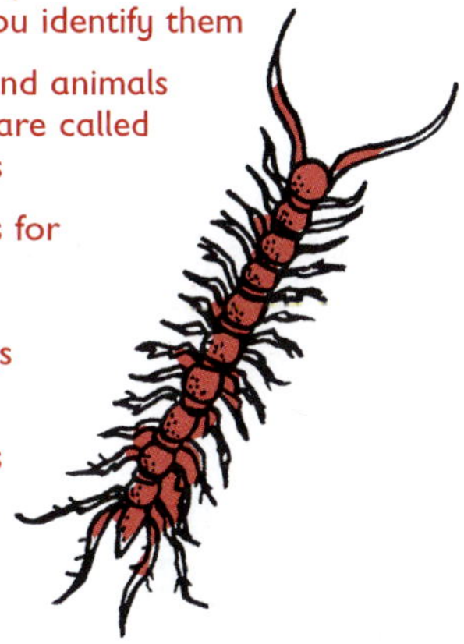

IDENTIFICATION BOOKS OR CDS may contain
- pictures
- descriptions
- information about where a plant or animal lives
- identification keys

use all these clues to help you decide if the identification is correct

IDENTIFICATION KEYS
- split a large group into smaller ones by asking questions
- can only be used to identify the plants or animals included in the key
- come in two types
  - branching keys – laid out as diagram
  - numbered keys – a series of numbered questions
- work best when made with questions that can be answered by either yes or no

- What do we mean by observable features of plants and animals? Describe two ways in which observable features can be used to help identify plants and animals. Use the chart to help you answer these questions.

Keep on track

Help your brain to remember things. Making up sayings or funny stories helps. Richard Of York Gave Battle In Vain is one example. It helps you remember the colours of the spectrum: red, orange, yellow, green, blue, indigo, violet. Make up your own.

Make up some revision games – for example, matching words and pictures on cards.

Try this!

Use magazine pictures of five famous people to make a key. Write down a question to split the group into two and then use other questions until you get down to groups of one. Questions like 'Is the person a woman?' or 'Is the person wearing glasses?' could be useful ones to ask. Can a friend use your key to identify the famous people? If so, your key works!

Grouping living things: classification

Keep on track

Cut out some pictures of different types of animals from magazines. Ask a friend to hold up each picture for 10 seconds. In the 10 seconds, try to say what group the animal belongs to and why.

How are you doing?

If you can use a key to identify living things, you are working at level 4.

If you can describe a wide variety of living things and can explain why classifying them is important, you are working at level 5. Well done!

- ✓ There are millions of different types of plants and animals on Earth.
- ✓ Scientists have worked out groupings for plants and animals.
- ✓ The grouping is based on features of the plants and animals.
- ✓ Knowing some of the main groups can help you to identify plants or animals you have not seen before.

LIVING THINGS → **can be put into groups depending on their features**
- this is called classification
- classifying plants and animals can help scientists decide how closely related they are

two of the main groups are:

GREEN PLANTS
- **don't move around**
- **make their own food using light energy**

  - flowering plants, e.g.
    – grasses
    – trees
  - non-flowering plants, e.g.
    – mosses
    – ferns

ANIMALS
- **can move**
- **take in food**

the main groups of animals are:
- molluscs, e.g. snails
- jellyfish
- starfish
- worms
- vertebrates (animals with backbones), sub-groups are:
  - fish, e.g. salmon, goldfish
  - amphibians, e.g. frog
  - reptiles, e.g. snake, lizard
  - birds, e.g. blackbird
  - mammals, e.g. human, dog, dolphin
- arthropods, sub-groups are:
  - insects
  - arachnids (spiders)
  - centipedes and millipedes
  - crustaceans, e.g. crab

- Use the chart to find the names of the five groups that the vertebrates (animals with backbones) are divided into. Choose one of the vertebrate groups and list as many examples of animals belonging to that group as you can think of. What are the features they all have in common?

Living things and their habitats: habitats

- ✓ The different types of places where plants and animals live are called habitats.
- ✓ Different types of plants and animals may be found in different habitats.
- ✓ Plants and animals are suited to live in their habitat. This is called adaptation.

HABITATS are PLACES where LIVING THINGS are found

must be able to find ENOUGH
- air
- water
- food
- shelter
- warmth

in their habitat to be able to survive

examples include
- FIELD
- WOOD
- POND
- SEASHORE

PLANTS
grass – can grow quickly, and is not killed if grazed
daisy – low growing, can stand being trodden on

ANIMALS
rabbit – eats grass seeds and shoots; can dig burrows
thrush – can probe into the soil to get worms

PLANTS
seaweed is fastened to rocks so it is not washed away

ANIMALS
crabs have hard shell to protect them from predators
seals can dive down to catch fish

the plants and animals are:
- **suited to their habitat**
- **depend on each other as well as the habitat to survive**

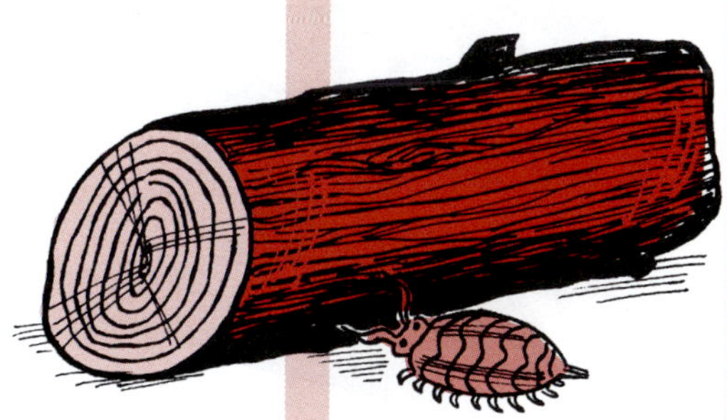

- Use the chart to identify the things a plant or an animal must be able to find in its habitat. Explain how a rabbit might be able to find all these things in its habitat.

Keep on track

Make some posters of key ideas and words. Change them every week or so.

Try this!

Look at a micro-habitat. Choose a small area of soil, a piece of rotten wood or a garden bush. Look very carefully to see how many different types of small animals live there. Try to decide how each one is adapted to the micro-habitat.

Living things and their habitats: food chains

Keep on track

Split up your work into small chunks. Don't try to revise too much at once.

Try this!

Humans can easily damage habitats and food chains. Do some research to find examples of places where people have damaged the environment and have affected food chains. Can you find an example where people have protected the environment?

- ✓ Plants and animals which depend on each other as food are called a food chain.
- ✓ Food chains start with a plant.
- ✓ Plants at the start of food chains are called producers.
- ✓ Food chains may have several animals.
- ✓ The animals are called consumers.

FOOD CHAINS

- **SHOW how animals use each other and plants for food**
- **start with PLANTS** — plants are called producers because they make food using carbon dioxide from air and water (see chart on page 14)
- **ANIMALS**
  - are called consumers because they eat or consume other living things
  - some animals only eat plants – they are called herbivores
  - some animals (called carnivores) eat other animals
    - animals which are eaten are called prey
    - animals which eat other animals are called predators
- **different food chains are found in different HABITATS**
  - **GARDEN** e.g. rose bush → greenfly → ladybird
  - **FIELD** e.g. grass → rabbit → fox
  - **POND** e.g. weed → tadpole → small fish → heron

- For one of the habitats on the chart, write out the food chain which is shown. Label the different living things in the chain as consumers, producers, predators, prey or herbivores. Some of them will have more than one label.

Life processes and living things

Living things and their habitats: micro-organisms

- ✓ Micro-organisms are living things which are very small. They cannot usually be seen without a microscope.
- ✓ Like other living things, micro-organisms feed, grow and reproduce.
- ✓ Some micro-organisms can cause diseases in humans and other living things.
- ✓ Some micro-organisms can cause food and other natural materials to decay.
- ✓ Some micro-organisms can be useful – for example, yeast in bread making.

MICRO-ORGANISMS

- **are sometimes called GERMS or MICROBES**
- **are VERY SMALL**
  - usually can only be seen by using a microscope
- **there are different TYPES**
  - bacteria
  - viruses
  - fungi, e.g. moulds and yeast
- **can cause some ILLNESSES**
  - colds
  - measles
  - chickenpox
  - this happens when they are passed from one person to another
- **can cause DECAY when they use a material as their food**
  - human food
    - **can go 'mouldy'**
    - **can be dangerous to eat if it has micro-organisms in it**
    - **should be stored and cooked so micro-organisms are not passed to people**
  - plant material, e.g leaves and wood
    - **is broken down by micro-organisms**
    - **this decay is helpful: it 'recycles' the plant material**
- **can be USEFUL**
  - yeast (a type of fungus) makes bread rise
  - micro-organisms are used to make yoghurt and cheese

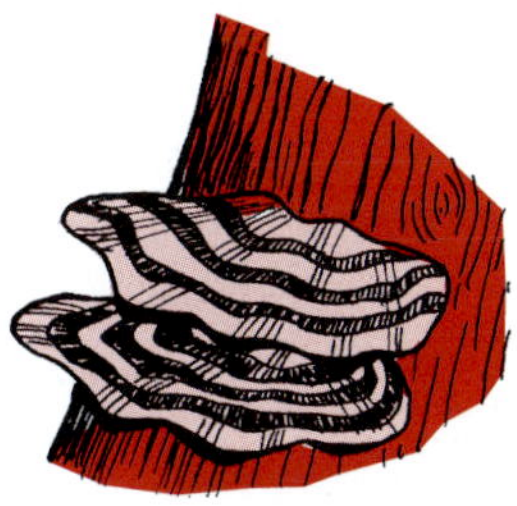

- Use the chart to make a table with two columns, one which shows the ways in which micro-organisms can be useful and one which shows the problems they can cause.

Keep on track

Use pages 19 to 21 to write two or three paragraphs about living things and their habitats. Then blank out some of the key words. Challenge a friend to fill in the spaces.

How are you doing?

If you can say how a particular animal is suited to its habitat (for example, a fish has fins so that it can swim in water), you are working at level 3.

If you can describe a food chain for a habitat, such as a field or a pond, and you can label the living things as producers, consumers, predators and prey, you are working at level 4. Well done!

Materials and their properties: uses

Keep on track

Don't revise for too long. Have a short rest every 10 minutes or so. Let your brain recover!

Try this!

Comparing papers
Paper has lots of different properties: for example, it tears, it soaks up water, it can be folded. How many more can you think of? Collect some sheets of different types of paper and decide on one property to test. Design a fair test to compare the papers.

- ✓ Different objects are often made of different kinds of material.
- ✓ Different types of material have different characteristics or properties.
- ✓ The properties of a material can make it suitable for certain jobs.

MATERIALS

- **come in different TYPES**
  - wood
  - metal
  - plastic
  - glass
  - paper
- **have certain PROPERTIES**
  - words are used to describe properties, each word usually has an opposite
  - hard/soft
  - flexible/stiff
  - transparent/opaque
  - strong/weak
  - waterproof/absorbent
- **of a certain type often have similar properties – for example, metals are usually**
  - shiny
  - strong
  - conduct electricity
- **are chosen for making OBJECTS or doing JOBS because they have properties which make them suitable**
  - windows – glass is used because it is transparent
  - roofs – tiles are used because they are waterproof
  - chair – plastic is used because it is strong but flexible

- Use the chart to pick out two different types of material. For each type of material write a list of words to describe its properties. Can you think of any objects that could be made from each type of material?

- ✓ Some materials let heat pass through quickly. They are called thermal conductors.
- ✓ Some materials only let heat pass through slowly. They are called thermal insulators.
- ✓ Materials that are good thermal insulators can be used to help keep things warm or cold.

MATERIALS

- which are good **THERMAL CONDUCTORS**
  - let heat pass through quickly
  - are mainly metals, e.g. copper, steel, aluminium
  - are usually good electrical conductors as well (see page 24)
  - can be a problem if they let heat pass to the wrong place, e.g. metal pan handles or spoons
  - can be useful if they let heat pass through quickly in the right place, e.g. radiators, saucepan bases
- which are good **THERMAL INSULATORS**
  - only let heat pass through slowly
  - include materials such as wood, plastic and wool
  - often trap small pockets of air, e.g. polystyrene, feathers, foam
  - have many practical uses
    - warm clothes
    - keeping houses insulated
    - keeping food warm or cold

- Use the chart to find a situation where a thermal insulator is useful. What material could be used in this situation?

Keep on track

Find a nice quiet spot to revise in. Don't have the television on, though background music might help.

Try this!

Ice cube competition
Make some large ice cubes in empty yoghurt pots. Put exactly the same amount of water in each pot. Half full is about right. Give each person in the competition an ice cube in a pot and allow them two minutes to find materials to insulate their pot. Check the pots after half an hour. The person with the biggest cube left is the winner! Why did their thermal insulation work best?

Grouping materials: electrical conductors and insulators

Keep on track

Ask someone to help you with your revision. He or she can test you by reading out questions.

Try this!

Materials that are electrical insulators are very important for electrical safety. Wires and switches that carry mains electricity are usually covered with plastic but they can get damaged. What would be your top five tips for keeping electrical insulation in good condition? What advice does your electricity company offer on electrical safety?

- ✓ Some materials let electricity pass through easily. They are called electrical conductors.
- ✓ Most electrical conductors are metals.
- ✓ Some materials do not let electricity pass through. They are called electrical insulators.

MATERIALS

- → **which let electricity through are called ELECTRICAL CONDUCTORS**
  - all metals are good electrical conductors
  - pencil lead (graphite) is an electrical conductor
- → **which do not let electricity through are called ELECTRICAL INSULATORS**
  - plastics are good electrical insulators
  - wood, glass and rubber are electrical insulators
  - insulators are used to protect people from mains electricity
- → **can be tested using a circuit with batteries and a bulb to see if they are ELECTRICAL CONDUCTORS** — if used to complete a circuit the bulb lights

  or

  ELECTRICAL INSULATORS — if used to complete a circuit the bulb will not light

- A class of children was testing objects to see if they were electrical conductors or electrical insulators. Some groups recorded that a pencil was an electrical conductor and some that it was an electrical insulator. Can you use the information in the chart to explain how this could happen?

- ✓ The Earth is made up of different kinds of rock. Sometimes the rock is hidden under a layer of soil.
- ✓ Different types of rock can be put into groups depending on their characteristics.
- ✓ Rock can be a useful material. Different types of rock are suitable for different jobs.
- ✓ There are different types of soil. This depends on the type of rock the soil comes from.

ROCKS

- **are found in different TYPES**
  - granite
  - marble
  - slate
  - limestone
  - sandstone
- **different types can be put into GROUPS**
  - by looking at their
    - colour – e.g. limestone is often white
    - shape – e.g. slate splits into flat sheets
    - texture, how rough or smooth they are – e.g. granite can be very rough
  - by testing their
    - hardness – by rubbing them
    - permeability – whether water soaks in
- **different types have different USES depending on their CHARACTERISTICS**
  - slate is used for roofs because it is flat and waterproof
  - granite is used for steps because it is very hard
  - marble is used for floors because it is hard and attractive
- **are found in small pieces in SOIL**
  - soil comes in different types
    - sandy
    - clay
  - the different types of soil depend on the type of rock found in them

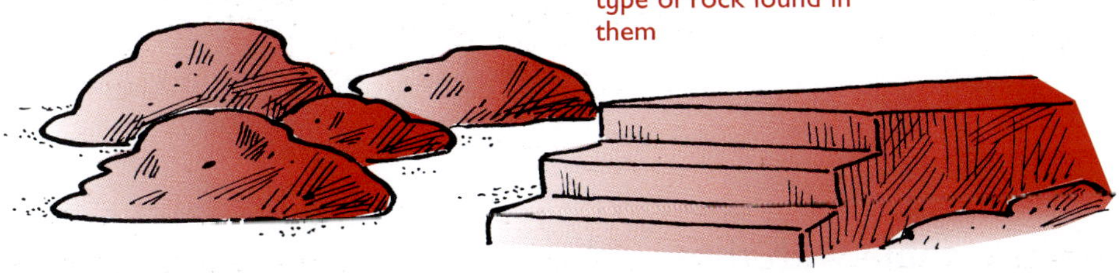

- Use the chart to write a list of characteristics of slate and a list of characteristics of granite. Can you add to the list from what you know about the uses of these rocks?

Keep on track

Use pages 22 to 25 to make a set of cards listing different types of material and another set showing different properties of materials. For each material pick three words which describe properties that the material has.

Try this!

Collect a small sample of soil and put it into an empty plastic drink bottle. Add some water, put on the top and shake the bottle. Leave it to stand for a couple of hours. How many different layers can you see? What do you think they are made of? Try some different samples of soil and compare the layers you get.

Materials and their properties

Grouping materials: solids, liquids and gases

Keep on track

Why not make your own revision card? Copy the main concepts of a topic on to some small pieces of card. You then can revise anywhere.

How are you doing?

If you can say why a material is suitable for particular jobs (for example, glass is used for windows because it is transparent), you are working at level 3.

If you can describe the differences between solids, liquids and gases using features such as their shape or how easily they flow, you are working at level 4. Well done!

Materials and their properties

- ✓ All materials can be put into one of three groups – solids, liquids and gases – depending on their characteristics.
- ✓ All solids have some similar properties.
- ✓ All liquids have some similar properties.
- ✓ All gases have some similar properties.

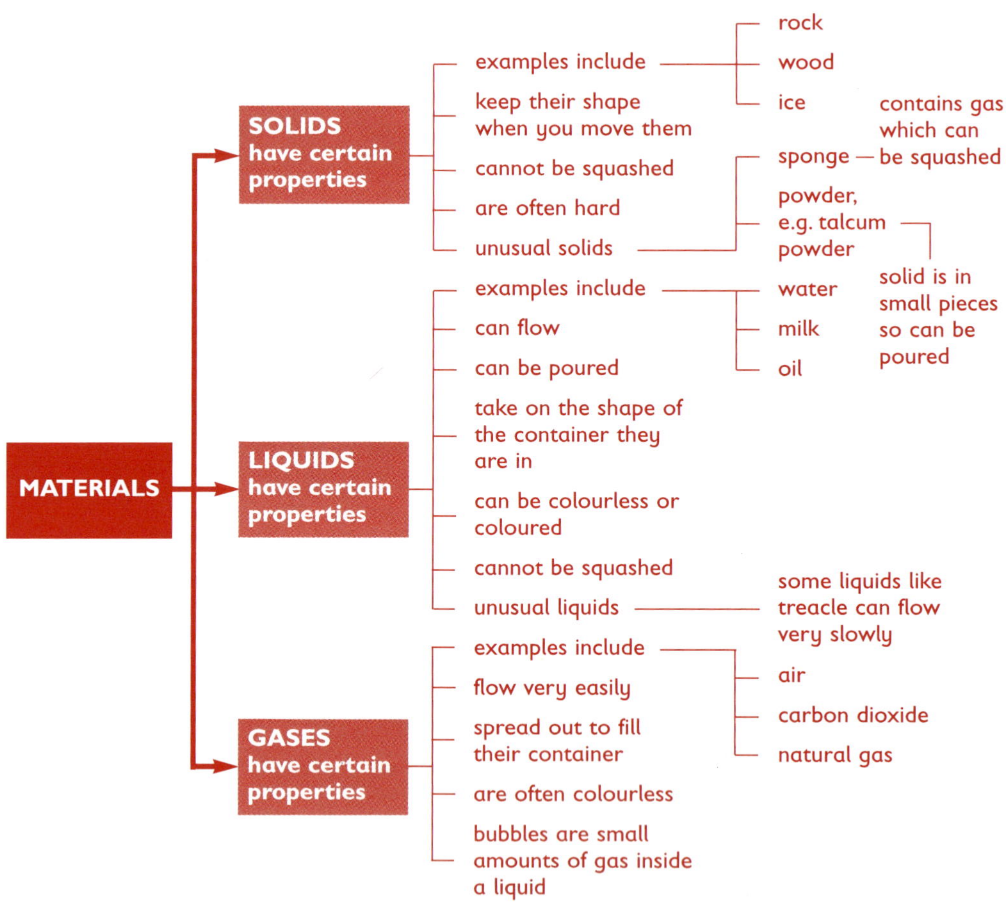

- Make a table with three columns headed solid, liquid and gas. Use the chart to help you fill in the main characteristics of solids, liquids and gases in the correct columns. Can you add any others?

- When two solids are mixed the two materials do not usually join together.
- Sometimes when a solid is put into a liquid the solid stays separate from the liquid. It does not dissolve.
- Sometimes when a solid is put into a liquid the solid mixes completely into the liquid. It dissolves.
- Sometimes when materials are mixed they join together to form a completely new material.

MIXING

- **SOLID WITH SOLID**
  - **the solids do not usually join**
  - **the two solids can both be seen in the mixture**
  - **the solid can usually be separated using a sieve (see page 34)**
  - **examples include sand with rice or sugar with peas**
- **SOLID WITH LIQUID**
  - **sometimes the solid DISSOLVES (see page 32)**
    - mixes completely into the liquid
    - can form a coloured or colourless liquid
    - solid can be separated by evaporation (see page 35)
    - examples include sugar and water, salt and water
  - **sometimes the solid DOES NOT DISSOLVE**
    - solid stays separate
    - solid can be separated by filtering (see page 34)
    - examples include sand in water, rice in water
- **sometimes makes NEW MATERIALS (see page 33)**
  - can happen with some solids and some liquids
  - you cannot usually separate the materials
  - examples include plaster of Paris and water or vinegar and bicarbonate of soda

- Use the chart to find the names of three methods that can be used to separate solids from different types of mixture.

Keep on track

Start your revision early. Don't wait until just before the tests!

Try this!

A healthy start
Breakfast cereal with raisins may be healthy, but what if you don't like raisins? Can you work out a way of separating them from the cereal without having to pick each one out?

Changing states: heating and cooling

Keep on track

Draw 'before and after' diagrams to show how different materials are affected when heated.

Try this!

We often heat up our food before we eat it. Cooking can make food taste better and can kill harmful micro-organisms on the food. However, some foods change when they are cooked. Make a list of some of the cooked foods you eat. Do they change as they are cooked? Are the changes reversible or non-reversible?

- ✓ Heating causes some materials to change.
- ✓ Some materials change back as they cool down.
- ✓ Some materials do not change back when they cool down.

HEATING

- **SOLID MATERIALS**
  - **some melt (turn into a liquid)**
    - melting is a reversible change
    - when melted materials cool down they turn back to a solid
    - examples include (see pages 29 and 31)
      - ice to water
      - candle wax to liquid wax
  - **some stay solid but change into a different material**
    - these changes are permanent or non-reversible
    - examples include (see page 33)
      - dough turns to bread
      - clay turns to pottery
- **LIQUID MATERIALS**
  - **some evaporate (turn into a gas)**
    - evaporation is a reversible change
    - when evaporated materials cool down they turn back into a liquid: they condense.
    - if liquids are heated strongly they can boil (see page 31)
    - examples include (see pages 29 and 31)
      - water to water vapour
      - perfume in a bottle to perfume in the air
- **SOME MATERIALS**
  - **can make them burn**
    - burning is a non-reversible change
    - flames come from the material
    - examples include (see page 33)
      - wood
      - natural gas
      - paper

- Changes that happen to materials when they are heated can be either reversible or non-reversible. Use the chart to find four examples of each kind of change.

Changing states: changes to water

- ✓ When ice is heated it turns to water. When water is heated it turns to water vapour or steam.
- ✓ When water vapour is cooled it turns to water. When water is cooled it turns to ice.
- ✓ Ice, water and water vapour are all the same material in a different state – solid, liquid and gas.
- ✓ Ice turns to water at a temperature called the melting point. Water boils to make steam at a temperature called the boiling point.

LIQUID WATER

- **when heated can turn to a gas by EVAPORATION**
  - the higher the temperature, the faster the water evaporates
  - water particles leave the surface of the water
  - water particles in the air form tiny droplets called water vapour
    - if water vapour cools it turns back to liquid water: this is called condensation
- **when heated strongly can turn to a gas by BOILING**
  - the water has to be heated quickly to boil
  - the water needs to reach its boiling point – a temperature of 100°C
  - bubbles of gas called steam form in the water
  - as steam leaves the surface it turns to water vapour
- **when cooled can turn to a solid by FREEZING**
  - water has to be cooled to its freezing point – a temperature of 0°C
  - water particles join together
  - the water turns into a solid called ice
    - if ice is heated it turns back to liquid water: this is called melting

- If some ice cubes were put in a pan and heated on a cooker, how would they change? Use the chart to help you describe the changes you would see.

Keep on track

It is easier to revise things you **understand**. So, if in doubt, go and ask someone to explain to you the ideas you don't understand.

Try this!

Quick-drying socks
Clothes dry as the water evaporates from them, but what conditions are the best for this? Collect four identical socks, dip them in clean water and put them in different places to dry. Use what you know about evaporation to predict the order in which the socks will dry.

Changing states: the water cycle

Keep on track

Draw the chart on this page. Cut out each block of writing and then try to reassemble the water cycle without looking at your book.

Try this!

Wet weather watch
Look at weather forecasts on the television or in newspapers for days when rain is predicted. Which parts of the country seem to get most rain? Can you link this to what you know about the water cycle?

- ✓ Water evaporates from the surface of the sea and lakes.
- ✓ Water vapour in the air condenses and falls as rain.
- ✓ Rain which falls over land flows down streams and rivers back to the sea.
- ✓ This complete process is called the water cycle.

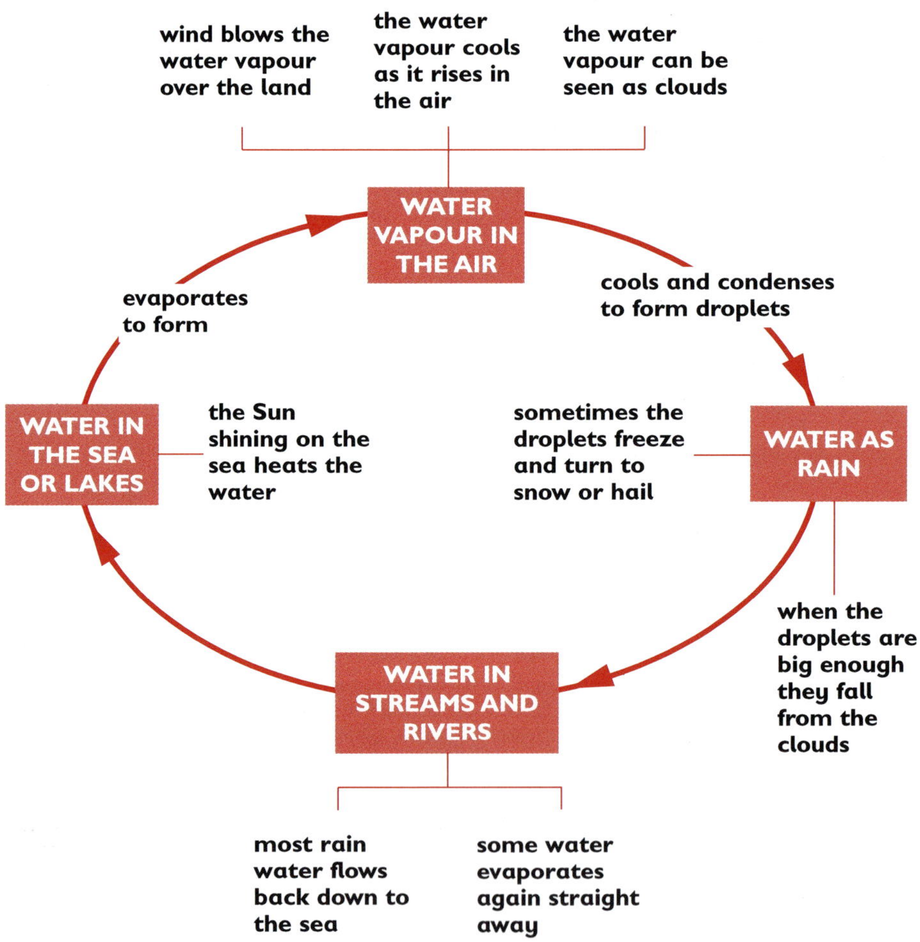

- For water to evaporate it has to heat up. For water vapour to condense it has to cool down. Use the chart to explain how these two processes happen in the water cycle.

- ✔ Like ice, some other solids melt to form a liquid when they are heated.
- ✔ Like water, some other liquids freeze to form a solid when they are cooled.
- ✔ Like water, some other liquids evaporate to form a gas when they are heated.
- ✔ Like water vapour, some other gases condense to form a liquid when they cool.
- ✔ These types of changes to materials are called changes of state. They are reversible changes.

HEATING

- **a SOLID can make it turn into a liquid. This change is called melting**
  - examples include – ice, candle wax, chocolate
  - the particles start to break apart
  - the temperature at which a material melts is called the melting point
- **a LIQUID can make it turn into a gas. This change can be**
  - examples include – water, perfume
  - **evaporation**
    - liquids evaporate at a range of temperatures
    - but the higher the temperature the faster a liquid evaporates
  - **and**
  - **boiling**
    - the liquid starts to bubble
    - the temperature at which a liquid boils is called the boiling point

COOLING

- **a GAS can make it turn into a liquid. This change is called condensation**
  - examples include – water vapour, natural gas
  - the gas particles join together to form drops of liquid
  - water condensation can be seen on cold surfaces such as mirrors or tiles
- **a LIQUID can make it turn into a solid. This change is called freezing or solidifying**
  - examples include – water, liquid candle wax, liquid chocolate
  - the particles in the liquid join tightly together as it freezes
  - the temperature at which a material freezes is called the freezing point

- Use the chart to find the names of the changes that can happen to materials when they are heated, and the names of the changes that happen when materials cool down.

Keep on track

Try to make your own summary page about each topic you study. This will help you bring together all the important ideas.

Try this!

Water freezes, but what about cooking oil and washing-up liquid? Ask a grown up for permission before you try this. Put small amounts of these liquids into empty yoghurt pots and cover the pots with cling film. Put the pots in the fridge for an hour. Does either liquid solidify? Now try them in the freezer.

Materials and their properties

Keep on track

Use pages 28 to 33 to find five examples of reversible changes and three examples of non-reversible changes.

How are you doing?

If you can give some examples of reversible changes (such as water freezing) and permanent changes (such as an egg cooking), you are working at level 3.

If you can use scientific words such as condensation and evaporation to describe changes to materials, you are working at level 4. Well done!

- ✓ When some solids are mixed with water they break down and become part of the liquid. This is called dissolving.
- ✓ The liquid made when a solid dissolves in water is called a solution.
- ✓ Dissolving is a reversible change.
- ✓ When some solids are mixed with water they stay as solids. They do not dissolve.

DISSOLVING

- some solids **WILL NOT DISSOLVE**
  - chalk
  - sand
  - glass
- some solids **WILL DISSOLVE**
  - sugar
  - salt
  - instant coffee
  - → the liquid is then called a **SOLUTION**
    - all solutions are clear (not cloudy)
    - some solutions have a colour
    - some solutions are colourless
- solids can be made to **DISSOLVE FASTER** by
  - breaking the solid into small pieces
  - using warm water
  - stirring the mixture
- dissolving is a **REVERSIBLE CHANGE**
  - you can get the solid back by evaporating all the water (see page 35)

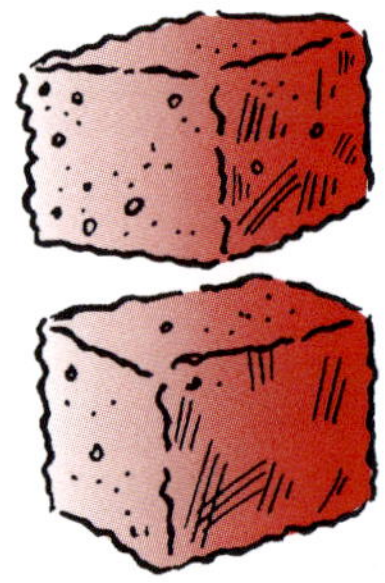

- Describe what you would see happening if you mixed a powder with water and it dissolved. Use the chart to help you.

Materials and their properties

- When materials change and they cannot be turned back into the original material, this is called a non-reversible change.
- Non-reversible changes happen when materials burn.
- Non-reversible changes happen to some materials when they are heated, even if they do not burn.
- Non-reversible changes happen to some materials when they are mixed.

NON-REVERSIBLE CHANGES

- **can happen when some materials are MIXED**
  - the materials react together
  - new materials are formed
  - if a new material is a gas, bubbles appear
  - the mixture may get hot
  - examples include
    - plaster of Paris and water
    - vinegar and bicarbonate of soda
    - lemon juice and washing soda
- **can happen when some materials are HEATED**
  - **some materials DO NOT BURN**
    - the heat causes the material to change
    - when it cools it does not change back
    - examples include
      - clay heated in a kiln turns to pottery
      - bread dough heated in an oven turns to bread
      - cake mixture heated in an oven turns to cake
  - **some materials BURN**
    - materials which burn are called fuels, e.g.
      - wood
      - wax
      - natural gas
    - to burn, materials need oxygen (a gas in the air)
    - when materials burn they give off heat
    - when materials burn you usually see flames and smoke
    - when materials burn new materials are formed, e.g.
      - ash
      - gases
      - smoke
      - (gases and smoke) these can be poisonous

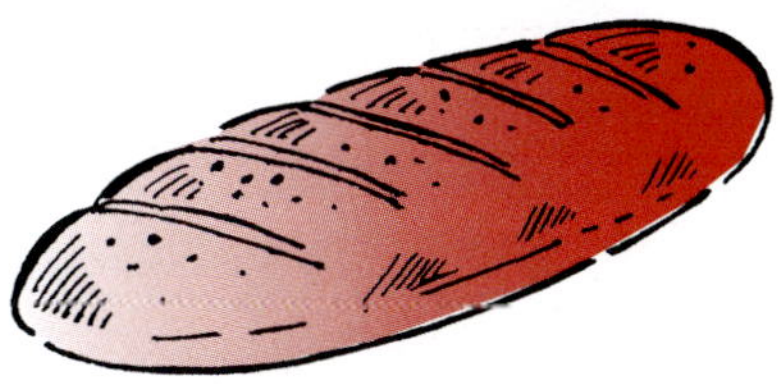

- Non-reversible changes produce new materials. Choose three examples of non-reversible changes from the chart and for each one explain how you would know that a new material had been made.

Keep on track

Don't just revise topics once. Keep coming back to them. Rereading will help you remember things.

Try this!

Fire safety
Fire in the wrong place can be very dangerous. It can cause burns and the smoke and gases given off are poisonous. Check out the advice given by your local fire service on fire safety in the home.

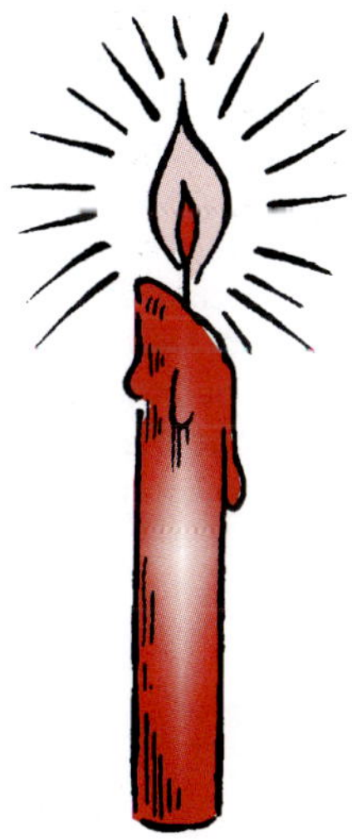

Materials and their properties

Separating materials: sieving and filtering

Keep on track

Why not draw up a timetable for your revision? This will help you to decide which topics to revise when.

Tick off sections on your revision timetable as you cover them. Aim to cover each topic at least twice before the tests.

Try this!

Which is the best filter paper? Collect sheets of four or five different types of paper. Fold each into a cone shape so you can pour some muddy water into it. Let the water collect in some empty yoghurt pots. Which paper gives you the clearest sample of water? What does this tell you about the size of the holes in the paper?

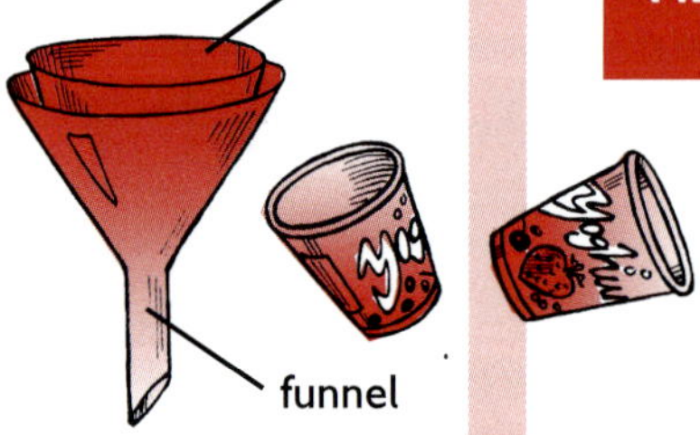

- ✓ Sieves and filters work in a similar way.
- ✓ Mixtures of solids can usually be separated by sieving.
- ✓ For sieving to work, the solids must be in different-sized pieces and the sieve must have the right size of holes.
- ✓ A mixture of a liquid and a solid which does not dissolve can be separated by using a filter.
- ✓ For a filter to work, it must have holes that are small enough for the liquid to pass through but not the small pieces of solid.

SIEVES — are used to separate **MIXTURES OF SOLIDS**
- the solids must be of different sizes
- the sieve must have the right size of holes
- shaking the sieve lets the smaller solids pass through the holes
- the larger solids stay in the sieve
- a mixture of several solids can be separated by using sieves with different-sized holes

FILTERS — are usually used to separate **MIXTURES OF SOLIDS AND LIQUIDS**
- the solid must be insoluble
- the filter is like a sieve with very small holes
- the holes may be too small to be seen
- the liquid flows through the holes but the solid stays in the filter
- paper and cloth can be used as filters
- everyday examples of filters include tea bags and coffee filters

- If you had a mixture of water, sand and glass marbles, how would you separate them? Use the chart to help you write down the steps you would go through in the correct order.

Materials and their properties

- When a solid dissolves in water, the particles of the solid mix completely into the solution.
- Even though the solid cannot be seen, the particles are still present in the solution.
- A solid which dissolves cannot be separated from the water by filtering.
- If the solution is left for some time the water will evaporate, leaving the solid behind.
- Evaporation can be used to separate a solid that dissolves from water.

SOLIDS

- **which DO NOT DISSOLVE in water can be separated by filtering (see page 34)**
  - examples include sand and glass beads
- **which DISSOLVE IN WATER form a SOLUTION**
  - examples include salt and sugar
  - the solid breaks down into small particles
  - the particles mix completely with the water
  - the solid particles cannot be separated by filtering — the particles are too small and go through the filter
  - when the solution evaporates, only the water particles escape into the air
  - the solid particles stay in the container
  - eventually only the dry solid is left

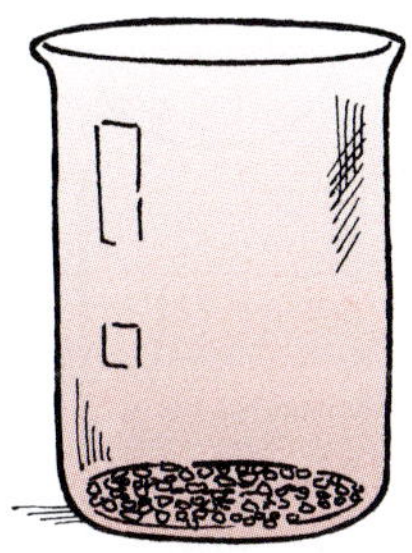

- If you had a mixture of water, sand and salt, how would you separate them? Using the chart to help you, write down the steps you would go through in the correct order.

Keep on track

Use the charts on pages 34 and 35 to draw labelled diagrams to show how sieving, filtering and evaporation work to separate materials.

How are you doing?

If you can describe how to separate mixtures that you have seen before, by using sieving, filtering and evaporation, you are working at level 4.

If you were given a mixture of a solid and a liquid that you had not seen before and could work out whether filtering or evaporation would be the best way of separating them, you would be working at level 5. Well done!

Keep on track

Ask someone to help you with your revision. He or she can test you by reading out the questions in this book.

How are you doing?

If you can look at this electrical circuit and say why the bulb is not working, you are working at level 3.

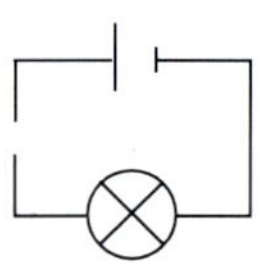

If you can draw a circuit diagram to show how an electrical device, such as a buzzer, has to be connected to work, you are working at level 4. Well done!

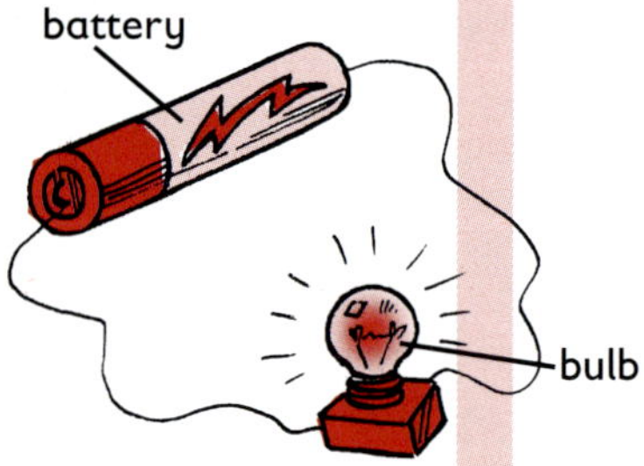

Physical processes

- ✓ Symbols are used to represent parts of electrical circuits and can be built up to make circuit diagrams.
- ✓ Circuit diagrams are easier and quicker to draw than pictures of circuits.
- ✓ Circuit diagrams can help you build circuits and understand how they work.

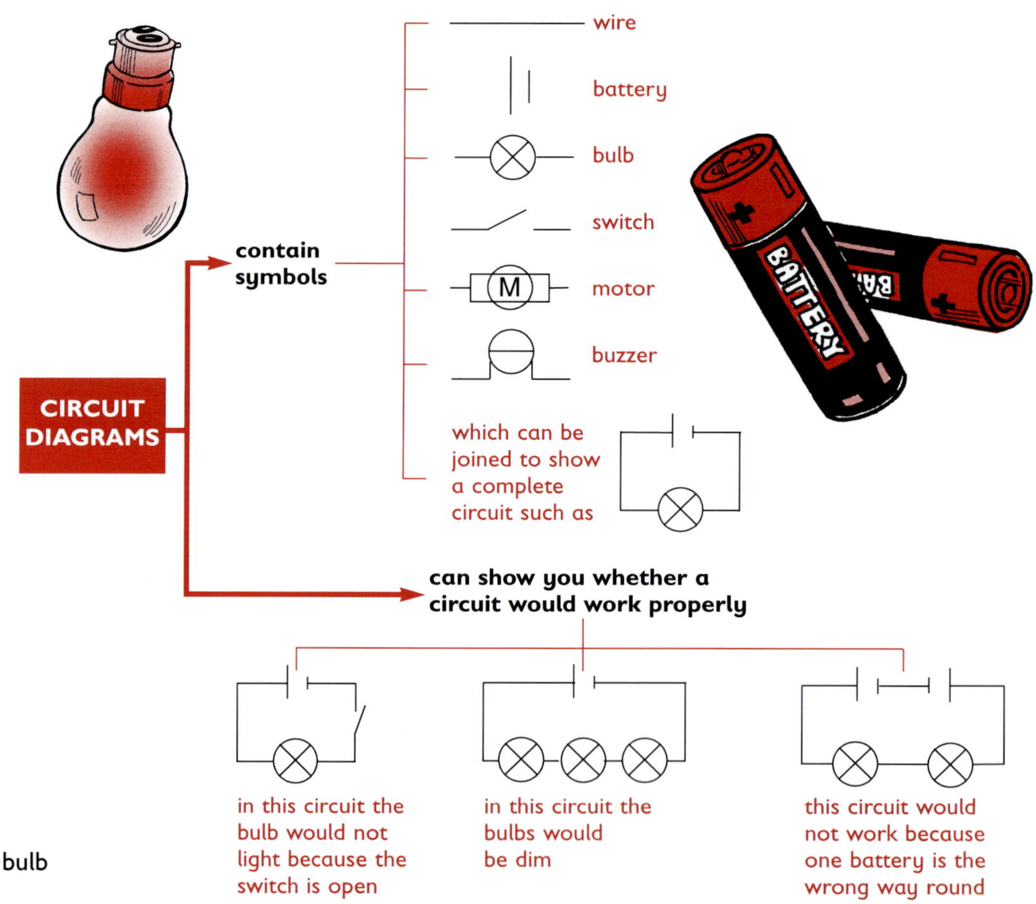

- Use the chart to help you draw circuit diagrams for these two circuits:
  - A circuit containing two batteries, a bulb and a buzzer.
  - A circuit containing a battery, two bulbs and an open switch.

- ✓ Only electrical circuits powered by batteries can be safely studied. Electrical equipment which works on mains electricity is dangerous.
- ✓ An electrical circuit will work only if the circuit is complete.
- ✓ An electrical circuit will work only if it includes an electrical power supply such as a battery.
- ✓ A switch works by making a gap in the circuit.
- ✓ An electrical circuit will not work if part of it is made of an electrical insulator. This idea can be used to test whether a material is an electrical conductor or an electrical insulator.

ELECTRICAL CIRCUITS

- **need the following things to work**
  - a complete circuit – one with no gaps and no parts made of an electrical insulator
  - a source of electricity such as a battery
  - an electrical device such as
    - – a bulb
    - – a buzzer
    - – a motor
- **can stop working when**
  - there is a gap in the circuit
    - this can happen if the circuit is broken
    - a switch is used to make a gap in the circuit
      - this can be used to turn the circuit on and off
      - this can stop electricity being wasted
  - part of the circuit is made of an electrical insulator – this can be used to 'test' electrical conductors and insulators (see page 24)
  - there is not enough electrical power
    - there are not enough batteries
    - the batteries are worn out
    - too many electrical devices have been put in the circuit

- You have made an electrical circuit that contains a battery, some wires, a switch and an electric motor. But when you press the switch the circuit does not work. How can you test the circuit to find out what is wrong? Use the chart to make a list of the things you should check.

Keep on track

Don't just read the work. Make your revision active by doing tasks such as changing the text into a diagram.

Try this!

Switches
All switches work by making a gap in an electrical circuit. But how many different types of switch can you spot around your home or at school? Are they used in particular places for a particular reason?

Physical processes

Keep on track

Practise test questions whenever you can. Use WHSmith's *National Tests Practice Papers*.

Try this!

Different batteries for different jobs

You can buy several different types of battery. Make a list of five electrical devices that use batteries. Look at the packaging of batteries in a shop to decide which type of battery would be best for each piece of equipment.

Physical processes

- ✓ Changing the type of bulb or type of battery used in a circuit can change the brightness of the bulb.
- ✓ Increasing the number of batteries in a circuit can make the bulbs brighter.
- ✓ Increasing the number of bulbs in the circuit can make each bulb dimmer.
- ✓ Using thinner wire in a circuit can make the bulb dimmer.
- ✓ Using longer wires in a circuit can make the bulb dimmer.

BULBS IN A CIRCUIT

- **can be made brighter by**
  - using a more powerful battery
  - using more batteries
  - using lower-voltage bulbs
  - using fewer bulbs
- **can 'burn out'** — if too much electrical power is used for them
- **must be 'matched' to the batteries used to work properly** — e.g. one 1.5 volt bulb with one 1.5 volt battery
- **can be made dimmer by**
  - using less powerful batteries
  - using fewer batteries
  - using higher-voltage bulbs
  - using more bulbs
  - using very thin fuse wire in the circuit — if a long length is used, the bulbs are even dimmer

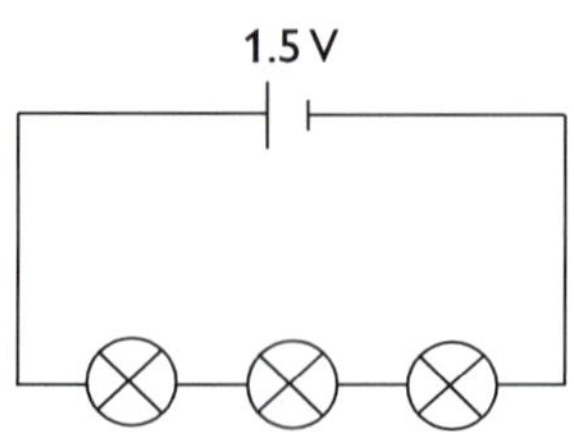

- You have made a circuit with three 1.5 volt bulbs and one 1.5 volt battery. The bulbs are very dim. Use the chart to work out two ways in which you could change the circuit to make the three bulbs brighter.

- Forces are pushes and pulls.
- When you push against something and squash it, it pushes back.
- When you pull on something and stretch it, it pulls back.
- Gravity is a force which pulls objects towards the centre of the Earth.

FORCES

- **can be 'pushes'**
  - which make things move
    - pushing a drawer shut
    - pushing down on a bike pedal
    - wheels pushing a car
  - which squash things
    - sponge
    - balloon
    - springs
      - push back when you squash them
      - the more they are squashed, the more they push back
- **can be 'pulls'**
  - which make things move
    - pulling a door shut
    - pulling a plug out of a socket
  - which stretch things
    - clothes
    - elastic band
    - springs
      - pull back when they are stretched
      - the more they are stretched the more they pull back
      - can be used to measure forces (see page 42)
  - gravity is the pull on an object towards the centre of the Earth
    - gravity causes objects to have weight
    - gravity is the force which makes objects fall

- Use the chart to help you make a list of objects which change shape when a force acts on them. What do all these objects have in common?

Keep on track

Try to make your own summary page about each topic you study. This will help you bring together all the important ideas.

Try this!

Stretchy tights
Use one leg of a pair of tights or a long sock to compare the pull of gravity. Peg up the tights and collect some objects which you can drop down the leg. Predict how much stretch each will produce as gravity pulls it down. Is there a pattern in your results?

Physical processes

Keep on track

Why not make your own revision cards? Copy the main facts of a topic on to some small pieces of card. You can then revise anywhere.

Try this!

Uses for magnets
Look around your home and at school for places where magnets are used. What uses do magnets have in industry? Try to find some information from books or on the Internet.

- ✓ When two magnets are brought close to each other, they either attract each other or repel each other.
- ✓ Magnets only attract some types of metal.
- ✓ Magnets do not attract any non-metal materials.

If a MAGNET

- **is put close to another magnet it will produce a force**
  - *either* attraction (the magnets pull together) *or* repulsion (the magnets push apart)
  - **the size of the force depends on how strong the magnets are**
- **is put close to a piece of metal**
  - what happens depends on the type of metal
  - sometimes the magnet attracts the metal — the metal is magnetic, e.g. iron, some steel, nickel
  - sometimes no force is produced — the metal is non-magnetic, e.g. aluminium, copper, gold
- **is put close to a non-metal material**
  - no force is produced — the material is non-magnetic, e.g. plastic, wood, paper
- **is put next to a non-metal with some iron behind it**
  - the magnet still attracts the iron
  - magnets can work through non-metals
- **is put next to a metal like aluminium with some iron behind it**
  - the magnet still attracts the iron
  - magnets can work through non-magnetic metals

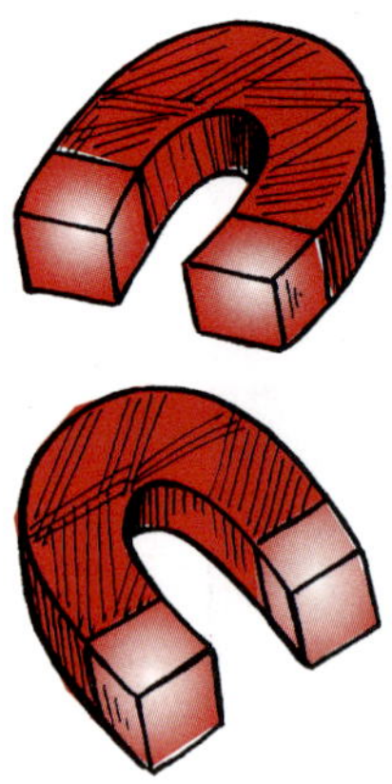

- Some coins look as though they are made of copper but they are attracted by magnets. Use the chart to help you explain how this could happen.

Physical processes

Forces and motion: friction

- ✓ When an object rubs on a surface, there is a force between the object and the surface called friction.
- ✓ The size of the friction can vary depending on the size of the object or the type of surface.
- ✓ When objects move through water or through air, they are slowed down by types of friction called water resistance and air resistance.
- ✓ Sometimes friction can be very useful – for example, bicycle brakes.

FRICTION

- **is a FORCE**
  - that happens when a moving object rubs against something
  - that slows down the moving object
- **happens between two surfaces**
  - for example, a wooden block pulled on:
    – carpet
    – plastic
    – wood
  - the size of the friction depends on the surface
  - smooth surfaces usually give low friction
  - rough surfaces usually give high friction
  - if surfaces are pushed together you get high friction
  - using a lubricant, e.g. water or oil, can reduce friction
- **which is HIGH can sometimes be useful** — for example: bike or car brakes, car tyres, soles of shoes
- **which is LOW can sometimes be useful** — for example: skis on snow, ice skates on ice
- **happens when an object moves through** — the size of water or air resistance depends on the shape of the object
  - **WATER** — this is called water resistance
  - **or through AIR** — this is called air resistance

- Bicycle brakes sometimes do not work as well in wet weather as in the dry. Use the chart to help you explain how friction is used in bike brakes and what happens in wet weather.

Keep on track

It is easier to revise things you **understand**. So, if in doubt, go and ask someone to explain to you the ideas you don't understand.

Try this!

Streamlined shapes
High air resistance can be useful: this is how a parachute works. But most forms of transport work better if they are streamlined (move through the air easily). See how many examples of streamlined shapes of vehicles you can spot in a day.

Keep on track

Draw some diagrams of everyday situations, using arrows to show the size and direction of the forces involved.

How are you doing?

If you can look at pictures like the ones below and say what the force will do to the object, you are working at level 3.

If you can explain how different types of forces affect how things move (for example, air resistance slowing a parachutist down, or oil reducing friction on a door hinge), you are working at level 4. Well done!

Physical processes

- ✓ Every force acts in a particular direction.
- ✓ The size and direction of forces can be shown on diagrams by using arrows.
- ✓ The size of a force can be measured using a Newton meter.
- ✓ When objects are put under water, the water pushes upwards on them. This force is called upthrust.
- ✓ Because of upthrust, when objects are suspended in water they seem to weigh less.

FORCES

- **on objects can be shown in diagrams by arrows**
  - the direction of the arrow shows the direction of the force
  - the longer the arrow, the larger the force
- **can be measured using a Newton meter**
  - Newton is the unit of force
  - Newton meters can be 'push' or 'pull' type
  - Newton meters have a spring inside them
  - the larger the force, the more the spring is squashed or stretched
- **on an object in air change when it is lowered into water**
  - gravity pulls the object down – this is called the weight of the object
  - in water, gravity still pulls the object down with the same force
  - water pushes up on the object with a smaller force called 'upthrust'
  - so the object seems to weigh less in water

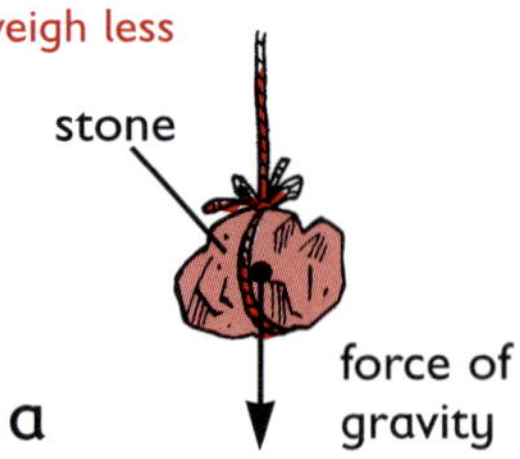

- The picture on the right shows a stone tied to a piece of string. The arrow shows the force of gravity pulling down on the stone. Draw a diagram to show the forces on the stone after it has been lowered into water. The chart will help you work out the size and direction of the forces.

- ✓ Objects which produce light are called light sources.
- ✓ Light travels away from light sources.
- ✓ Shadows are formed when an object blocks the light travelling from a light source.
- ✓ When light from the Sun is blocked, the shadows formed change during the day.
- ✓ Some objects let most light pass through them, but they may still form faint shadows.

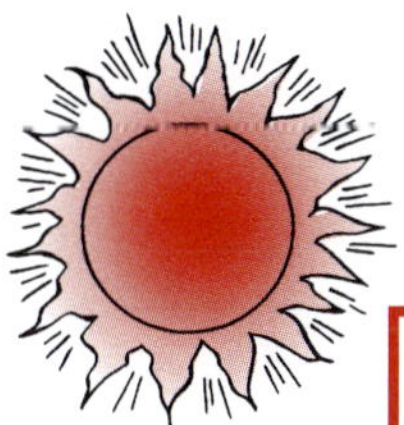

LIGHT

- **is produced by some objects**
  - examples include the Sun, light bulbs, candle flames
  - these objects are called sources of light
  - light travels away from these objects
- **is blocked completely by some objects**
  - examples include wood, cardboard, stone
  - these materials are called opaque — **OPAQUE OBJECTS**
    - produce dark shadows
    - the shadow is a similar shape to the object – this is because light does not bend round the object
- **passes through some materials**
  - examples include glass, some plastic, ice
  - these materials are called transparent — **TRANSPARENT OBJECTS**
    - may block a small amount of light
    - produce faint shadows
- **from the Sun makes shadows that change during the day** (see page 47)
  - get longer and shorter
  - get darker and lighter
  - change position

- Use the chart to find an example of an opaque material and an example of a transparent material. Think of an object made of each of these materials. Draw each object and the shadow you think it would make if it were placed in front of a bright light source.

Keep on track

Use the topic charts in this book to help you. They will show you how different ideas link together.

Make some posters of key ideas and words. Change them every week or so.

Try this!

Shadow shapes

Use a torch and some opaque objects to investigate what effect changing the angle of the light has on the shape of the shadow. What angle gives a shadow which is most like the shape of the object?

Physical processes

Light and sound: light

Keep on track

Don't just revise topics once. Keep coming back to them. Rereading will help you remember things.

Try this!

Exploring reflections
Look at your reflection in a mirror. What happens if you put your right hand up? Place some objects in front of the mirror. What colour are the reflections? What happens to writing in front of a mirror? Make a list of the things that stay the same in reflections and the things that change.

Physical processes

- ✓ We see objects when light coming from them enters our eyes.
- ✓ Some objects produce light. They are light sources.
- ✓ Some objects reflect light.
- ✓ Shiny objects reflect light better than dull objects.
- ✓ When light is reflected from an object it changes direction.

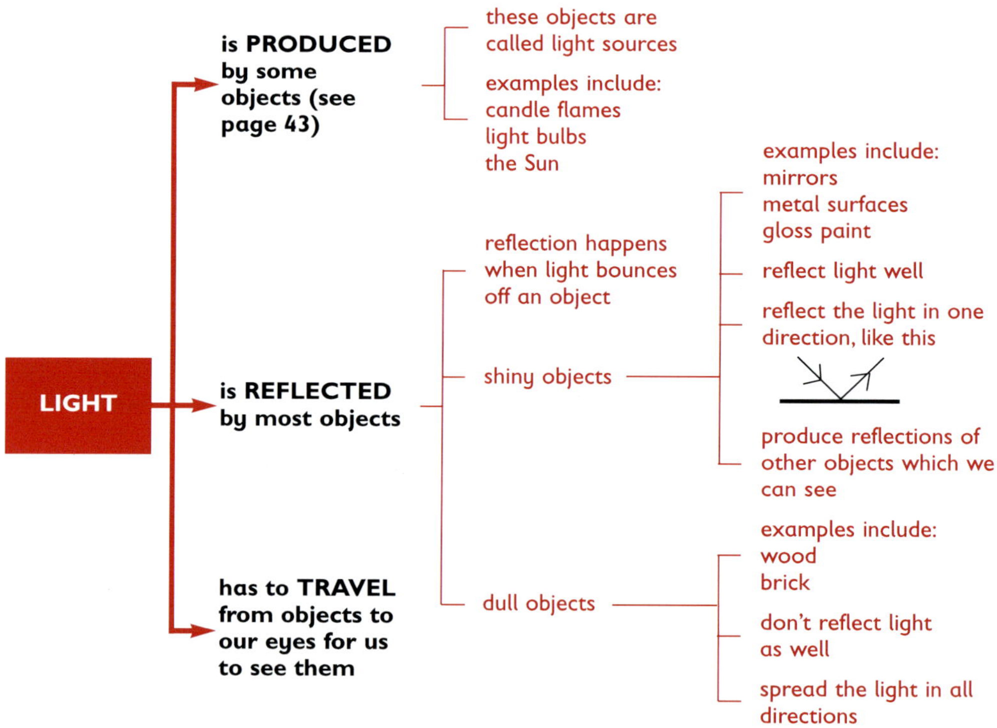

- Use the chart to help you draw two diagrams:
  - A diagram to show how you can see light from a candle flame.
  - A diagram to show how you can see writing on a page of a book.

Use lines with arrows to show how the light travels.

- Sounds are made when objects vibrate.
- Vibrations travel through air and other materials to reach our ears.
- Some materials can muffle the vibrations and reduce the sound.

SOUND

- **is made when an object VIBRATES**
  - objects which produce sound are called sound sources
  - hitting or shaking an object can make it vibrate
  - sound vibrations are usually too small to see
  - you can do things to see the vibrations in some objects
    - put a tuning fork in water
    - put pieces of paper over strings
    - put rice on a drum
- **TRAVELS through materials to reach our ears**
  - sound usually has to travel through air
  - the vibrations get fainter the further away they travel
  - sound can travel through liquids
    - sound in swimming baths
    - whale songs underwater
  - sound can travel through solids
    - sound through walls
    - sound along central heating pipes
    - string telephone
  - some materials muffle sound – they absorb the vibrations (see page 46)

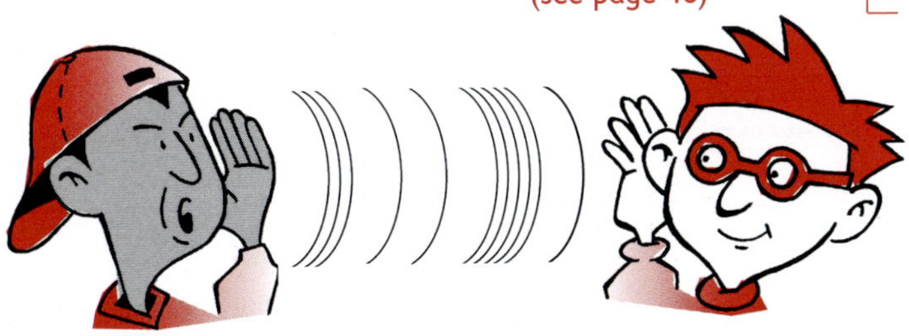

- Sound vibrations usually reach our ears by travelling through the air, which is a gas. What evidence is there that sound can travel through solids and liquids as well? Use the chart to find some examples of each. Can you think of any more?

Keep on track

Make up some questions to test your friends with – this helps you to understand the ideas involved.

Try this!

Good vibes
Collect some different rubber bands and stretch them over an empty plastic margarine box. Pluck the bands. Which band gives the highest note and which gives the lowest note?

Put some small folded strips of paper over the bands. Can you see the vibrations? Put a few grains of rice or sand in the margarine tub. Can you see vibrations there?

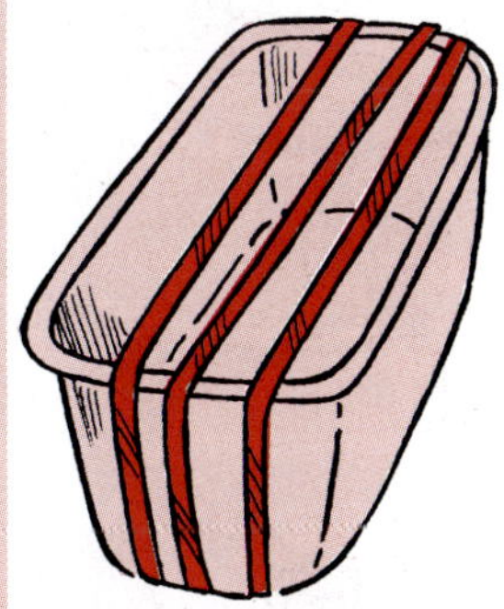

Light and sound: sound

Keep on track

Use the information on pages 43 to 46 to write a list of five things light and sound have in common and five things that are different about them.

How are you doing?

If you can describe how a sound will change as you get further away from the object making the sound, you are working at level 3.

If you can describe by using diagrams what is happening to the light when we see an object such as a book, showing where the light comes from and how it gets to our eyes, you are working at level 5. Well done!

Physical processes

- ✓ The pitch of a sound is how high or low the note is.
- ✓ The pitch of the sound made by a musical instrument can be changed.
- ✓ The loudness of the sound made by an object depends on the size of the vibrations.
- ✓ Some materials are good at absorbing sound vibrations.

CHANGING SOUND

- **PITCH**
  - high notes
  - low notes
- **MUSICAL INSTRUMENTS**
  - drums
    - higher pitch
      - smaller drum
      - tighter skin
    - lower pitch
      - bigger drum
      - looser skin
    - louder
      - hit harder
      - hit in the middle
  - strings, e.g. guitar
    - higher pitch
      - thin strings
      - shorter strings
      - tighter strings
    - lower pitch
      - thicker strings
      - longer strings
    - louder
      - plucked harder
  - wind, e.g. recorder
    - higher pitch – shorter tube
    - lower pitch – longer tube
    - louder – blow harder
- **REDUCING NOISE**
  - some materials absorb sound
    - thicker materials reduce sound more
    - good materials include carpet, foam rubber, wool

- The drums in a band are too loud for the other instruments. Describe three ways in which you could make the drums quieter. Use the chart to help you.

- The Earth spins once every 24 hours and this causes day and night.
- During the day the Sun seems to move across the sky, but really this is caused by the Earth turning.
- The changing position of the Sun in the sky causes changes to shadows.

THE EARTH

- **spins once every 24 hours**
- **turning causes day and night**
- **has different parts facing the Sun at different times**
- **turning makes THE SUN *seem* to move across the sky**
  - rises in the east and sets in the west
  - is highest in the sky at noon – shadows are shortest
  - is lowest in the sky at sunrise and sunset – shadows are longest
    - the pattern of shadows during a day can be seen by pushing a stick into the ground and observing the shadow at different times

- Using the chart to help you, draw some diagrams of a shadow stick showing how the shadows would change between sunrise and sunset. One has been done for you.

Keep on track

Make up some revision games – for example, matching words and pictures on cards.

Try this

Changing seasons
The Sun always rises in the east and sets in the west but how high it seems to get in the sky and how long it shines for change at different times of year. Use books or CDs to research why this happens. Are seasons the same everywhere on the Earth?

Physical processes

The Earth and space: Earth, Sun and Moon

Keep on track

Make a diagram to show five key facts each about the Earth, the Sun and the Moon.

How are you doing?

If you can explain why the Sun seems to move across the sky during the day, you are working at level 4.

If you can set up a model using a torch for the Sun and balls of different sizes for the Earth and the Moon, and can use the model to show the phases of the Moon, you are working at level 5. Well done!

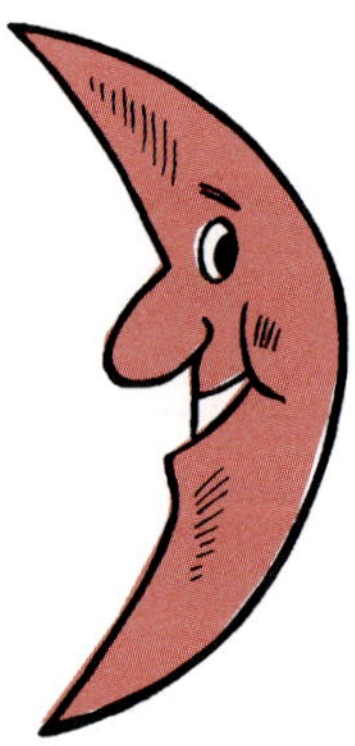

- ✓ The Earth, Sun and Moon are all spheres.
- ✓ The Sun is many times bigger than the Earth and the Earth is bigger than the Moon.
- ✓ The Earth orbits (goes round) the Sun: one orbit takes a year.
- ✓ The Moon orbits the Earth: one orbit takes 28 days.
- ✓ How much of the Moon you can see changes as it orbits the Earth.

THE EARTH
- **orbits THE SUN**
  - is like a ball in shape – a sphere
  - is a star
  - is about 150 million km from Earth
  - is a light source
  - is many times larger than Earth
- **is a sphere**
- **spins on its axis every 24 hours** — this causes day and night
- **takes one year to orbit the Sun**

THE MOON
- **is a sphere**
- **is much smaller than the Earth**
- **takes 28 days to orbit the Earth**
- **reflects light from the Sun**
- **looks different at different stages in the 28-day orbit**
  - full Moon — the Sun shines fully on the Moon
  - 'new' Moon — no Sun shines on the Moon

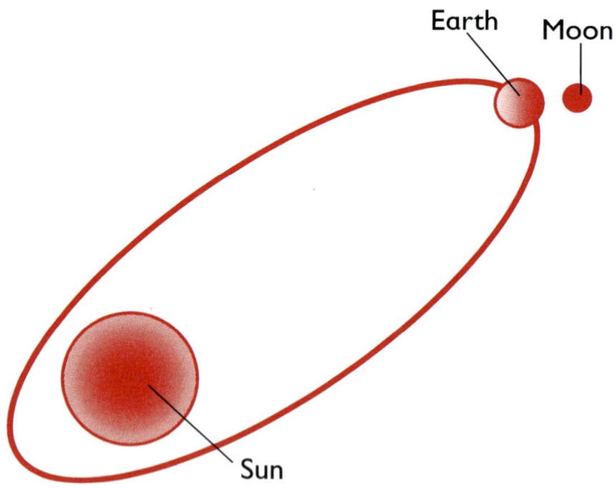

- Use the chart to help you make a list of the things that the Earth, the Sun and the Moon have in common, and a list of the ways in which they are different.

Physical processes